The ABC's
of TRUTH

The ABC's
of TRUTH

*Speaking Truth in
a Culture of Lies*

J. Lindsay Sadler, Jr.

XULON PRESS

Xulon Press
2301 Lucien Way #415
Maitland, FL 32751
407.339.4217
www.xulonpress.com

Scripture quotations taken from the English Standard Version (ESV). Copyright © 2001 by Crossway, a publishing ministry of Good News Publishers. Used by permission. All rights reserved.

Scripture quotations taken from the New American Standard Bible (NASB). Copyright © 1960, 1962, 1963, 1968, 1971, 1972, 1973, 1975, 1977, 1995 by The Lockman Foundation. Used by permission. All rights reserved.

Paperback ISBN-13: 978-1-66282-062-5
Ebook ISBN-13: 978-1-66282-063-2

DEDICATION

A huge thank you to my wife and John Deizo, our lawyer, for editing my manuscript. In addition, this book is dedicated to my children, grandchildren, nieces, and nephews. My heart aches for them to know truth and not be deceived by the culture's lies.

TABLE OF CONTENTS

INTRODUCTION

M artin Luther, the father of the Reformation (1517), stated, "If you want to change the world, pick up your pen and write."[1] Because my heart aches for the confusion, intolerance, lies, and violence in America over truth, I have felt a great burden to take Luther's advice. Someone once said, "In a war, truth is the first casualty."[2] Instead of living with a Christian undergirding, many in our nation have abandoned God as the Truth, and they are living from their fleshly opinions, desires, and experiences to manufacture a truth. This opponent of truth is truthiness. Throughout the book, the word "truthiness" is used to describe false teachings. Merriam-Webster Dictionary defines the word as "the belief or assertion that a particular statement is true based on the intuition or perceptions of some individual or individuals, without regard to evidence, logic, intellectual examination or facts."[3] If someone

---

[1] Jaquelle Growe: http://www.jaquellecrowe.com.

[2] Quote Investigator: https://quotinvestigator.com.

[3] Merriam-Webster : July19,2008, http://www.merriam-webster.com/dictionary/mondegreen

disagrees with a person's truthiness, then he cannot be in his life circle, and those who won't buy into the stated truth will be stereotyped, marginalized, and possibly persecuted.

Truth vs. truthiness leads to the second aspect of the book—tolerance vs. intolerance. Bakers, florists, and photographers have been penalized for not serving homosexual weddings. In 2013, the New Mexico Supreme court ruled against Elane Photography in Elane Photography v. Willock. The Christian couple who owned the photography business was told to compromise their religious beliefs in order to be good American citizens. One justice wrote, "It is the price of citizenship."[4] Where is tolerance or justice in this case? Why couldn't they just agree to disagree? Despite the fact that the suing couple found a photographer much cheaper, they still decided to pursue their so-called intolerant adversaries. It would appear the court had no convictions as they found the photographers guilty of engaging in discriminatory business practices.

Many of the chapters in the book deal with my third purpose for writing the book: engagement vs. apathy. Where are the Christian voices raised to bring truth to a culture deceived by lies? Dietrich Bonhoeffer, pastor during Hitler's reign, said, "Not to speak is to speak. Not to act is to act."[5] The church is God's army to engage in the spiritual warfare playing out in our world today. She is not to be silent and apathetic toward

---

[4] https://albertmohler.com: 2013/08/26:it is the price.

[5] https://www.goodreads.come: Bonhoeffer quotes.

truthiness and intolerance by hiding behind her stained-glass windows, ignoring the battle for truth raging outside those windows. It is the responsibility of the Christian to stand up for truth in our culture and not wait for someone else to do it.

Finally, as we engage in this battle for truth, we see the lines drawn between facts and feelings. We must live our lives in the reality of facts and not feelings. Feelings can be misleading, manipulated, and manufactured to lead a person down a road of delusion, disappointment, and destruction. Feelings do not lead a person to truth or tolerance; facts do.

Who is behind all the confusion in America? The father of lies—Satan. John 8:44 reads, "You belong to your father, the devil, and you want to carry out your father's desires. He was a murderer from the beginning, not holding to the truth, for there is no truth in him. When he lies, he speaks his native language, for he is a liar and the father of lies." We have politicians, pastors, news reporters, and media commentators often skirting the truth, basing their reporting on feelings and opinions, not facts. Their deceptive words are used to fuel the feelings of confusion, anger, and/or hate. They are being used to fulfill Satan's strategy. His scheme is to divide. Satan knows if he can divide a family, a business, a country, he wins. The commander-in-chief of lies recruits into his army anyone who is promoting lies. The old military adage is true, "Divide and conquer."

With truth at war with truthiness, tolerance battling intolerance, the Christian's engagement versus Christian apathy, and facts competing with feelings, we must be prepared to bring hope to a world through the inerrant truth of Scripture. It is my heartfelt desire that in these pages you will find encouragement to speak the truth of Jesus to a dying world.

ABSOLUTENESS OF THE TRUTH

"Without truth we are all vulnerable to manipulation."[6] Oz Guinness

"Therefore, Pilate said to Him, 'So You are a king?' Jesus answered, 'You say *correctly* that I am a king. For this I have been born, and for this I have come into the world, to testify to the truth. Everyone who is of the truth hears My voice.' Pilate said to Him, 'What is truth?' And when he had said this, he went out again to the Jews and said to them, 'I find no guilt in Him'" (John 18:37-38).

T he battle in America's culture today is determining who is telling the truth. Like Pilate, people are asking what is truth? Is CNN or Fox News telling their audiences the truth? Which newspapers are telling the truth? Is everyone spinning

---

6 Os Guinness, *Time for Truth: Living free in a world of Lies, Hype, and Spin*, (Grand Rapids, Michigan, Baker Books, 2,000), p. 82.

the story or facts to satisfy their moral or political views? Are Democrats or Republicans telling the truth? Sad to write, but which church is telling the truth—churches that hold to the inerrancy of Scripture, or those who do not?

For a society to flourish, absolute truth, not truthiness, must be woven into the culture's fabric. Otherwise, everybody is susceptible to being maneuvered toward the loudest voice.

Jesus is the Truth (John 14:6), not a truth. He came to give an anchor of absolute truth. The Truth came from outside of this world to give His creation a clear road map of life—no sideroads, exits, dead ends, expressways, but a narrow path of the Truth of how to have satisfaction in life (Matt. 5:6, 6:33, 7:24-27). However, like Pilate, it is foreign to most to say there is absolute truth. Consequently, society is scratching its head trying to figure out who is telling the truth. Jesus stated, "For this I was born and for this I have come into the world, to bear witness to the truth" (John 18:12). The truth problem is solved through Jesus Christ. He is the One broadcasting TRUTH.

Everyone has to answer these questions about creation, the fall, and redemption respectively:

1) How did it all begin? How did I come into existence?
2) What happened? Why all the chaos in the world?
3) How can it be corrected? Who can put it back together?

The answer to creation, the fall, and redemption is found in Jesus. All things were created by Him and for Him (Col. 1:16). Sin came into the world through the disobedience of Adam and Eve, which has created a chaotic world (Gen. 3). To correct the fall of man, God came into the world in the person of Jesus Christ (John 1:1, 14). He came to pay for our sin debt by nailing our sins to His cross (Col. 2:13-14).

Which is true to answer these basic questions: Is Jesus the absolute Truth, or is it Satan who can twist truth (truthiness) to manipulate others toward the unbiblical lies regarding creation, sin, and redemption?

Francis Schaeffer said in his 1981 speech at Notre Dame, "Christianity is not a series of truths in plural, but rather with a capital 'T.' Truth about total reality, not just religious things. Biblical Christianity is Truth concerning total reality and the intellectual holding of that total truth and then living in light of the truth." [7]

Jesus cleared up Pilate's question, "What is truth?" All who hear and obey the voice of Jesus will know the Truth, and they will not fall prey to the manipulators.

QUESTIONS TO CONSIDER

Do you believe there is absolute truth? If not, why?

---

[7] Nancy Pearcey, *Total Truth: Liberating Christianity from Its Cultural Captivity* (Wheaton, Illinois, Crossway Books, 2004), p.16.

What is the source of absolute truth? Is it science, opinion, news reports, or the Bible?

Have you ever been in a situation of manipulation? If yes, how did you feel, and how did you react?

THE BIBLE IS THE TRUTH

We must "be utterly convinced that there is a biblical perspective on everything – not just spiritual matters."[8] Nancy Pearcey.

All truth must begin with God. We capture His truth through the Bible. There is the secular worldview of life, and then there is the biblical or Christian worldview. The two views have clashed over the centuries, but only one can be correct.

Not surprising, the inspired Word of God states it is truthful. "You are near, O Lord, And all Your commandments are truth. The sum of Your word is truth, And every one of Your righteous ordinances is everlasting" (Ps. 119:151, 160). Church is not about traditions or worship styles but about whether or not the inerrant and trustworthy Word of God is preached. Albert Molher, President of Southern Baptist Theological Seminary, in Louisville, Kentucky, wrote the following:

---

[8] Nancy Pearcey, *Total Truth: Liberating Christianity from Its Cultural Captivity* (Wheaton, Illinois, Crossway Books, 2004), p.33.

Luther tried to go back to the first century and
understand the essential marks of the church,
and the first mark he listed was preaching.
Where the authentic preaching of the Word
takes place, the church is there, he said. By contrast, where it is absent, there is no church. No
matter how high the steeple, no matter how
large the budget, no matter how impressive the
ministry, it is something other than the church.[9]

Due to the various views of Scripture, there is confusion over which church is preaching and teaching truth.
For example, one church teaches women can be pastors or
instructs the gay community that God created its sexual ori-
entation, and another church does not. Some churches teach
"theistic evolution," and other churches hold to the "intelligent
design" instruction. Which church is telling the truth?

In my first church, a young man went off to college and
entered into the gay lifestyle. His parents called and asked me
to visit their son on campus. I scheduled a meeting with the
student. During our time together, I presented the scriptural
view of homosexuality and why it was not in agreement with
his lifestyle. He listened intently, but upon finishing my argument, he simply said, "Pastor, I talked to an Episcopal priest,

---

[9] R. Albert Mohler, Jr., *A Passionate Plea for Preaching: The Primacy of Preaching,* (Orlando, Florida, Reformation Trust Publishing, 2008, 10.

and he said it was fine to live this way." In seconds, my apologetics went up in flames.

Reason in our culture has overtaken revelation. For thousands of years, the Word of God has stood the test of time. However, in America, human reason has become the idol of the land. We can live as we choose, lie if necessary, spin facts, and say or do whatever is necessary for our agendas to come to fruition. This is truthiness—speaking and living without any factual undergirding or with only minimal truth wrapped in one's opinion.

Theologians, pastors, and teachers have exercised theological gymnastics to twist the Scriptures to appease a movement or a worldview. The church's biblical authority has been silenced.

Who is telling us the truth, the Bible or the culture? More times than not, when churches and so-called Christians muffle the Bible, their speech blends into the culture's voice. Thus, Scripture is no longer a player in any argument. The church's teachings and the Christian's voice become a faint whisper.

Truthiness has infiltrated society's thought process more than the trustworthiness of Scripture. The seventh president of the United States, Andrew Jackson, stated, "The Bible is the rock on which our Republic rests."[10] Another president, Abraham Lincoln, called the Bible, "The best gift God has given to man. But for it, we could not know right from

---

[10] https://www.axquotes.com:Andrew Jackson

wrong."[11] As Nancy Pearcey wrote, "Be utterly convinced that there is a biblical perspective on everything – not just spiritual matters."[12] Sadly, there are only a few who are convinced.

QUESTIONS TO CONSIDER

If the Bible is truth, what makes it true?

Is Luther's statement true today? "If the Word is not preached, the church is no longer the church."

What would you do if your pastor and/or church taught anything that went against Scripture?

---

[11] https://www.goodreads.com: Abraham Lincoln

[12] Nancy Pearcey, *Total Truth: Liberating Christianity from Its Cultural Captivity* (Wheaton, Illinois, Crossway Books, 2004), p.33.

Church – The Upholder
of "True-Truth"

"If I profess with loudest voice and clearest expo-
sition every portion of the truth of God except
precisely that little point which the world and
the devil are at that moment attacking, I am
not confessing Christ, however boldly I may
be professing Christ. Where the battle rages,
there the loyalty of the soldier is proved, and to
be steady on all the battlefield besides is mere
flight and disgrace if he flinches at that point."
[13]Francis Schaeffer

Late Christian apologist Francis Schaeffer termed truth,
"true-truth" to communicate that truth was absolute, not
relativistic. When the truth is voiced in culture, the truth
causes truthiness devotees to coil like rattlesnakes to strike
back. Why? Their humanistic influence is being threatened.
Humanism teaches that man is the measure of all things. The

---

[13] https://www.thegospelcoalition.org: Be Where the Battle Rages

church has been designated by God to represent the kingdom of God, Who is the measure of all things, not humanism. As the late Chuck Colson stated, "The Church is to make the invisible kingdom of God visible."[14]

Kingdom-of-God people have been transformed to acclimatize to their new residence through their repentance of sin and their faith in the substitutionary atoning work of Jesus's cross and His resurrection. Christians should have become accustomed to a new environment, the kingdom of God, by coming under the authority and rule of God. Having been acclimated to the kingdom-of-God life, the church has been set apart to "umpire" the world (Col. 3:15). In the text, "rule" means to umpire. When pseudo-truths are obvious, the church is to blow the truth whistle to call foul. By the Lord's grace, the church is empowered to carry out heaven's ordained task of upholding TRUTH through the power of the Holy Spirit and the living Word (Heb. 4:12).

To young Timothy, the apostle Paul wrote the clarion call to the church then and now, "If I delay, you may know how one ought to behave in the household of God, which is the church of the living God, **a pillar and buttress of the truth**" (1 Tim. 3:15). The church is to be the "umpire" and support, or foundation, of the truth. As Schaeffer stated, "If the Church winks at untruth, then the Church is not confessing Christ."[15]

---

[14] https://www.lightsource.com: Make the Invisible Kingdom Visible – Chuck Colson, Daily Devotion

[15] https://www.thegospelcoalition.org: Be Where the Battle Rages.

With that said, are churches that endorse same-sex relationships or turn a blind eye to cohabitating couples or are silent on the abortion issue really churches? If the church does not uphold the inerrancy and the trustworthiness of Scripture, is the church the church?

Our country is in a truth war. The battle is fierce, and the casualties are increasing. In light of the war in the land, the church has lost her wartime identity in the culture. All of the churches that dot the landscape in America are to be fortresses of the truth. Sadly, the church is composed mostly of swimmers being swept away by the ocean's undertow of lies and manipulation, moving them away from the truth.

Most churches have sheathed their weapon, the Word of God. They have abandoned the truth for a social agenda and liberal, philosophical sermons which pull the church into the powerful undertow of the culture's pseudo-truths. Many worship and praise a God they don't even know; then they leave worship believing all is right in the land.

If churches do not change their passive identity of being a sanctuary of truthiness to a bastion of truth, America will be turned over to human reason, which will slam the door on "true-truth." Eventually, America will become a dry and barren land because the Word of the Lord has **not** been buttressed by churches (Amos 8:11).

Questions to Consider

How can the church "umpire" the culture?

Has the church morphed into the culture, or has the culture morphed into the church?

Is there more philosophical preaching today or exegeting Scripture from the pulpit?

DISCOVERING THE TRUTH

"Man's love of truth is such that when he loves
something which is not the truth, he pretends
to himself that what he loves is the truth, and
because he hates to be proved wrong, he will
not allow himself to be convinced that he is
deceiving himself. So, he hates the real truth
for the sake of what he takes to heart in its
place." (St. Augustine, *Confessions*)

God has already created all things, and mankind is on a
journey of discovering how things function and how
life progresses. Discovering God's truth creates a culture of
the truth. Science, medicine, philosophy, inventions, and biblical truth are all based on discovery. The conclusion is that
nothing is created but discovered.

Our culture, however, is a pseudo-truth manufacturer. The
end product of a false truth is created around one's opinion,
which is solidified through feelings, desires, or experiences. It
matters not if there are no legitimate facts to back the opinion;

the outcome is a politically correct (PC) verbiage and life-style. At one time, it wasn't PC to say, "Merry Christmas" in the public square; one had to say, "Happy Holidays." In addition, many churches use the acrostic r.e.s.t. (reason, experience, Scripture, tradition) to interpret the Bible. More times than not, reason and experience trump Scripture. This is why these churches believe that homosexuality is not a sin. When America's Supreme Court in June 2015 bulldozed traditional marriage, it established a cultural truth and a church truth based on, in large part, the weight of public opinion and reason. When there is no biblical worldview, the humanist view of the world can be decreed by the powerful or influential few.

The second president of the United States, John Adams, stated, "[W]e have no government armed with power capable of contending with human passions unbridled by morality and religion ...Our constitution was made only for a moral and religious people. It is wholly inadequate to the government of any other."[16] In Scripture, Peter said, "Many will follow their sensuality, and because of them the way of the truth will be maligned" (2 Peter 2:2). If everything is relative, based on one's opinion from his desires or experiences, then any idea, lifestyle, religious, or political thought can become a truth. What the apostle Peter wrote centuries ago applies to twenty-first-century people.

What isn't addressed in cultural relativism is human sin. The selfish independent nature of each person really desires

---

[16] https://www.brainyquote.com: John Adams – Our Constitution.

to be on stage. Pride has a boastful side and a pitiful side. The boastful use power to manipulate. The pitiful actors have a suffering attitude that tugs on the heart-strings of others. The homosexual community, the immigration issue, and other social issues all are shouting, "Poor pitiful me; it's not fair!"

With pride on the heart's stage, the logical conclusion is that anyone can produce his own truth through personal discovery. Desires, feelings, and experiences are the factory workers to create satisfaction and an acceptable view of oneself. A pseudo-truth comes off the factory assembly line packaged to say, "I'm right." So, how many new pseudo-truths will be fashioned this year from the cultural truth factory? Remember, any manufactured truth has a shelf-life. These false truths will eventually fade, especially when America is in bondage by the government or another nation. Then, hopefully, people will begin digging to discover, not create, golden nuggets of the truth.

Lay down the burden of needing to create a truth to satisfy a feeling or desire. Close your truthiness factory and discover Jesus—the TRUTH.

Questions to Consider

Moral truth is discovered, not created. How does one discover moral truth?

Is it true that the Constitution can only be successful with a moral people?

S.I.N. – Selfish Intendent Nature is cloaked in pride—pride of being boastful and pride of the poor, pitiful me. Which cloak of pride do you wear or wear the most often?

EVAPORATION OF THE TRUTH

"The sleight of the tongue has the Truth vanishing before our eyes."[17] Unknown

"Let the lie come into the world, even dominate the world, but not through me." [18]Aleksandr Solzhenitsyn

T he sleight of the tongue from liberal, humanistic, relativistic thinkers dominates America's truth base. These slick talkers of pseudo-truth, or truthiness, will eventually cause the demise of America because the influence of these few have usurped the truth. Consequently, complicity of the people will be expected and enforced. The truth is fading away in all cultural arenas. For example, the pseudo-truth advocates, the government, and liberal churches have supported the mandate that the public-school systems must teach evolution. Our

---

[17] Os Guinness, *Time for Truth: Living free in a world of Lies, Hype, and Spin*, (*Grand Rapids, Michigan, Baker Books, 2,000*), p.60.

[18] Ibid., p. 19.

children are being taught that transgenderism is an accepted lifestyle and they have to sort out feelings of which gender they want to be. The twisting of the truth has kept the unborn life in jeopardy. Homosexual indoctrination is also in the educational pipeline. History is being altered by teaching that 1619, not 1776, was the beginning of America. The Critical Race Theory (CRT) is being promoted in our educational system as well. The Heritage Foundation states, "CRT makes race the prism through which its proponents analyze all aspects of America life and CRT underpins identity politics which is an effort to reimagine the United States as a nation driven by groups."[19] The vanishing of the truth extends from the tender age of a kindergartener through college. As history has proven, the liberal thinker will lead America to the brink of a Marxist ideology—a movement toward socialism that could evolve into communism. The church has lapsed into a theological coma allowing "true-truth" to disappear. When the truth is abandoned, the most formidable voices will change the landscape.

The Bible teaches that the Christian is not to be carried away or held captive to the philosophies of the world (Col. 2:8). Scripture warns the church that there are false teachers. Plus, there is a strong reminder not to worship idols (1 John 5:21). In light of the current cultural worldview, how does the Christian worldview proponent respond to those who are working to evaporate the truth from American society?

---

[19] Htttps://www.heritage.org: progressivism

From the teachings in the Beatitudes, the Christian response is obvious (Matt. 5:2-12). Jesus was instructing that when you take the Christian character into the culture, a crisis will occur. The crisis will result in persecution from proclaiming the name of Jesus and that He is the only way to heaven (John 14:6). Even though suffering will come with the truth, the Christian's motivation is to make "true-truth" reappear like a rainbow after a rain storm.

Violence in the nation won't allow the truth to reemerge in America. The transformed life gives the Christian grace in the battle of ideas to combat the false teachers. The apostle Paul wrote, "To speak truth in love" (Eph. 4:15). To young Timothy, he wrote, "With gentleness correcting those who are in opposition, if perhaps God may grant them repentance leading to the knowledge of the truth" (2 Tim. 2:25). Jesus and Stephen, as they were taking their last breaths, said, "Forgive them for they do not know what they are doing" (Luke 23:34; Acts 7:60). Early in His ministry, Jesus taught that His followers were to "love your enemies" and to "pray for those who persecute you" (Matt. 5:44).

If the truth is our treasured possession and we want the truth to resurface in our land, then all Christians need to cease living a fragmented or a compartmentalized life. The Christian community must heed Solzhenitsyn's statement, "Let the lie come into the world, even dominate the world, but not through me."[20] The Christian must speak and live the

---

[20] Ibid., p. 19.

truth in the land of lies with boldness, but wrapped in an attitude of agape love, to combat truth evaporating from our land.

QUESTIONS TO CONSIDER

If evolution is a theory and creation is a fact, which is true?

Which do you listen to for advice, the philosophies of the world or Scripture?

How will living out the Beatitudes change your lifestyle?

FREEDOM IN THE TRUTH

"Truth without freedom is a manacle, but freedom without truth is a mirage."[21] Os Guinness

From the garden of Eden until now, humankind was to live within certain boundaries. God told Adam and Eve not to eat from the tree of the knowledge of good and evil for they would die. When they believed Satan's lie that they wouldn't die, they learned death is a certainty, birth pain is a reality, and making a living is a labor of intensity (Gen. 3:16-19). When we are free to fulfil our wants, desires, and emotions without the guardrails of the truth, then sin is free to make life miserable.

The truth has little to no freedom to be expressed without opposition by the liberal to leftist positions that control the country. In my city, a Republican has little to no freedom to voice an opinion or be on the city council because the Democrats of the town rule, and they won't allow an opposing

---

[21] Os Guinness, *Time for Truth: Living free in a world of Lies, Hype, and Spin*, (Grand Rapids, Michigan, Baker Books, 2,000), p.87.

voice to weigh in on the conversations or decisions. Jesus challenged the Pharisaical religious position. His freedom to teach the truth was shut down by them. So much so, they argued for and won His crucifixion. In America today, people of the truth are being stifled or handcuffed by being tagged as irrelevant, foolish, narrow-minded, and worse.

Many teenagers yearn to be free from their parents' rule. Then in adulthood, they quickly learn that their freedom is limited. They are bound to the laws of the land, the requirements of their employer, and, if married, the responsibilities of a family. Broken laws, slackness or finding a new job in the workplace, and an affair or divorce are all escape mechanisms from feeling restrained and unfulfilled. This is why the divorce rate is high, suicides have increased, and there are many substance abuse cases that lead to various addictions. True freedom, Guinness wrote, is expressed through historian Lord Acton, "Freedom is not the power of doing what we like but the right of being able to do what we ought." [22]

Jesus made it clear where freedom originates, "If you abide in My word, you are my disciples indeed. And you shall know the truth, and the truth shall make you free" (John 8:31-32). In John's second epistle, he rejoiced that many walked in truth by keeping the commandments (2 John 4-6). Likewise, in 3 John, he again rejoiced that God's children were walking in truth (vv 3-4). Then in verses 9-12, he compared Diotrephes with Demetrius. Diotrephes was not walking in truth but in

---

[22] Ibid., p.86.

his fleshly pride, whereas Demetrius had a good testimony from the truth. One was free; the other was trying to find freedom in himself. Everything outside of Jesus is sin and places one in bondage.

Without the truth, there is no real freedom, and humankind can only live out of its sinful flesh. The truth gives security, significance, and satisfaction. The boundary lines are drawn by the Word of God, and by staying within the boundaries, significance is created from within. One knows that the Lord is pleased and glorified. When security and significance lock arms, then satisfaction of life wells up within the person. All of this occurs because the truth is free to complete its work.

The realization must be that there is no true freedom without the truth, only an imagined desert oasis where freedom is lost in pseudo-truths. Many think they have pitched their tents in that beautiful desert oasis, when one day, they will realize it is empty of everything but scorching sun and dry sand.

Questions to Consider

Are you really free without truth?

Do you see living in boundaries as good, or do boundaries shackle you?

How does Lord Acton's statement set with you? "Freedom is not the power of doing what we like but the right of being able to do what we ought."

GOD OF THE TRUTH

"Into Your hand I commit my spirit; You have ransomed me, O Lord, God of truth" (Psalm 31:5).

"'You are My witnesses,' declares the Lord, 'And My servant whom I have chosen, So that you may know and believe Me And understand that I am He. Before Me there was no God formed, And there will be none after Me'" (Isaiah 43:10).

"...for you shall not worship any other god, because the LORD, whose name is Jealous, is a jealous God" (Exodus 34:14).

"In hope of eternal life, which God, who never lies, promised before the ages began..." (Titus 1:2).

T he introductory Scripture texts proclaim two facts about God: First, He is the God of truth. Second, He is the only God. The psalmist sang out correctly, "O LORD, our Lord how majestic is your name in all the earth" (Psalm 8:1). David, the psalm writer, said Yahweh, God's name, then gave God's title, Lord, which means Adonai or Sovereign One. God is majestic in that He is all sovereign, all satisfying, and all sufficient. If He is "all," then He is the one and only God who is truthful.

The Apostle Paul to Titus was right in saying God never lies. All that He teaches from Genesis to Revelation is true. The forty authors of the sixty-six books, who were inspired by the Holy Spirit, wrote what God instructed them to write. God gave them no errors, constrictions, or half-truths.

Being a God who is majestic and truthful, He demands allegiance and obedience. As Exodus 34:14 says, God is a jealous God. He does not want to be, and will not be, in competition with other man-made gods. John Calvin wrote that the heart of man is an idol factor.[23] One of the major themes in Scripture is idol worship. We turn our hearts away from the true God thinking our god will satisfy. When Moses went to Mount Sinai to receive the Ten Commandments, upon his return, he found that the Israelites had created a golden calf to worship (Ex. 32). God was ready to destroy them, but Moses pleaded for Him to relent. God did so, but He sent a

---

[23] https://www.goodreads.com: John Calvin.

plague upon the people (Ex. 32:35) as punishment for their disobedience.

In a world of pluralistic faith views, which faith is telling the truth? The most accepted answer to the question is that all views will one day lead to God and/or heaven. If God is a jealous God, can that be true? Other faith gods demand a works righteousness to please the god, and each of these faiths operates out of duty in order to attain heaven.

The God of Christianity, Yahweh, desires His followers to delight in His goodness and grace, and as a result, the individual's aim will be to produce good works. If one knows Jesus and abides in His words, then he will know the truth, and the truth will set him free (John 8:31-32). The key is to know that good works will not earn one enough credits to get into heaven. God's grace is the only credit needed to reach heaven, which comes through Jesus's imputing righteousness to the believer (2 Cor. 5:21). Jesus made it abundantly clear how to go to heaven; it is only through Jesus that one can come to the Father or heaven (John 14:6).

The only way one will realize that the God of Christianity is the only true God is to be born again or regenerated. Good works will not create a new heart, religious traditions will not, nor will rule keeping. Only by the grace of God will one know the truth, that God is Truth—God the Father, Son, and Holy Spirit (Eph. 2:8-10).

Isaiah was correct in his text; there is no god before or after the Triune God of the Bible. This must be pondered. How about you? Are you searching for the God of truth, or will you remain satisfied with your idols?

Questions to Consider

Can God lie? If so, why would He lie?

If He doesn't lie, why can't you trust Him?

Why are man-made gods dead and the Christian God still living?

HOLY SPIRIT OF THE TRUTH

"When the Helper comes, whom I will send to you from the Father, *that is* the Spirit of truth who proceeds from the Father, He will testify about Me" (John 15:26).

"But when He, the Spirit of truth, comes, He will guide you into all the truth; for He will not speak on His own initiative, but whatever He hears, He will speak; and He will disclose to you what is to come" (John 16:13).

The above texts reveal three truths. First, the Spirit comes from the Father. Second, the Spirit speaks on behalf of the Father. Third, the Spirit is a Person. Again, what separates Christianity from other faiths is that God lives in the believer through the Person of the Holy Spirit. The Spirit becomes the primary teacher for the student of Jesus. Everyone is taught by someone. For example, a parent teaches his children racism. A child doesn't become racist; he is taught prejudicial behaviors.

A parent fuels the sinful nature, which causes the child to express his pseudo-truth. The Holy Spirit, however, always leads the believer into truth.

The gift of the Holy Spirit, the third person of the Trinity, gives believers the advantage (John 16:7) over the world, the flesh, and Satan's temptations. Having this advantage, Christians can know biblical truth to discern if public opinion mirrors this truth and discern right from wrong when the fleshly desires want to be satisfied and when Satan throws a temptation in front of a believer, knowing biblical truth keeps the believer on the safe path of righteousness.

The Holy Spirit acts like an umpire in a baseball game. His rule book is the Bible. When an act is performed that doesn't line-up with the Scriptures, the Holy Spirit calls an out. Every day, the believer is challenged by the sinful trio (the world, flesh, and Satan). Their goal is to convince you that lies are truth and will bring lasting peace. But in reality, they want your life to be depressing, unfulfilling, and not satisfying so you will always be looking for the next best thing to bring you pseudo-peace. The Holy Spirit, in concert with the Word of God, teaches truth. Before every action taken, every opinion expressed, or any lifestyle undertaken, it needs to be filtered through the Word of God. Then the Holy Spirt will be the wise teacher and counselor to guide you. Because the Holy Spirit is a Person, He can be "quenched" (1 Thess. 5:19) by believers dishonoring the Lord, which causes Him to "grieve" (Eph. 4:30). The Holy Spirit's primary desire is to bring glory to Jesus (John 16:14), and He does so by pointing the believer to glorify God.

Some faiths don't acknowledge the Holy Spirit or any spirit. Others mischaracterize Him as a force, not a Person. Again, the resurrection fulfilled the Old Testament and Jesus's teachings of the promise that a Helper would come to testify to the truth (Ezek. 36-37). Jesus was very clear during the Last Supper when He said that He must go to the Father so the Holy Spirit would come.

Most people are wandering in a desert of self-centeredness trying to discover truth. Sadly, they are looking for life's answers in all the wrong places. When mankind tries to sort through information and so-called facts without the Holy Spirit's leading, the default is almost always toward the sinful desire, resulting in the heart manufacturing idols, pride, covetousness, and a lying spirit, which does not lead to glorifying God. Life's answers are not found within self but beyond themselves through the Holy Spirit, Who desires to live within people. The Holy Spirit has empowered all who follow Jesus to know truth, to share truth, and to live the truth.

QUESTIONS TO CONSIDER

The Holy Spirit is what: a force, a Person, or doesn't exist?

What does the Holy Spirit work with to teach a believer?

When the Holy Spirit is quenched, then He grieves; how does that affect a believer?

INDOCTRINATION IN THE TRUTH

"Christians embrace a theology of the cross, not a theology of glory."[24] Martin Luther

"...[5] You shall love the Lord your God with all your heart and with all your soul and with all your might. [6] These words, which I am commanding you today, shall be on your heart. [7] You shall teach them diligently to your sons and shall talk of them when you sit in your house and when you walk by the way and when you lie down and when you rise up. [8] You shall bind them as a sign on your hand and they shall be as frontals on your forehead. [9] You shall write them on the doorposts of your house and on your gates" (Deuteronomy 6:5-8).

---

[24] Https://www.baptistnews.com: Falwell and Luther: a theology of glory verses a theology of the cross.

The short interpretation of the above text is to teach the household the truth of God. As Luther stated, a Christian worldview is a theology of the cross, not a theology of one's glory. A theology of the cross is one that bids a follower of Jesus to come and die. To understand the Christian faith, one must die to self. Jesus was clear—if His followers wanted to find life, they had to lose their lives (Matt. 10:39, 16:25). A Christian is to take up his cross daily, deny himself, and follow Jesus (Matt. 16:25). As John the Baptist stated, "He (Jesus) must increase, but I must decrease" (John 3:30).

Applying the truth of the cross to the family, parents should be diligent about teaching their children the ways of Christianity. Parents are diligent about vaccinating their children but laissez-faire about the world's indoctrinating them with a secular philosophy. Most parents encourage their children to get a liberal education and allow them to choose their faith belief system. Some even allow the child to choose his gender. So many households are unknowingly throwing their children into the jaws of a secular worldview, a worldview which states that mankind is god and life is to fulfill my desires. Yet, these parents are totally unaware of the consequences that their children will experience. Solomon wrote in Ecclesiastes that all is vanity and most are just chasing after the wind. He wrote about the vanity of wisdom, self-indulgence, work, and other life issues. At the end of the twelfth chapter, he concluded that the equation of life has to include God—fear God and keep His commandments (12:13a).

When rearing children, a family needs to attend a church that believes the Bible is inerrant, but also, the parents must teach and live the Word in the home. They are to teach that all have sinned and fall short of the glory of God (Rom. 3:23). As John Newton wrote, "Man's two greatest needs are to know that he is a great sinner and Christ is great Savior." [25] The tragedy is either the parents rear the child in a liberal church or no church or their own walk with the Lord is immature. Without a solid biblical foundation from their parents, many teenagers after receiving a driver's license or achieving graduation will never darken a church door again.

Therefore, biblical indoctrination must be a staple in the family as it will provide true instructions for the most satisfied life.

The apostle John wrote to the church in Ephesus (Rev. 2), who had lost its first love, to do the following: remember, repent, and return. Remember God's goodness and grace in life. Then repent from not loving God foremost in life. And finally, return to godly deeds of the faith. It is through returning to an indoctrination of the truth that a family will discover joy and peace in life and a secure future. Families will see their children handling life skillfully for the glory of the Lord.

---

[25] https.//www.goodreads.com: John Newton

Questions to Consider

To follow Christ, one must die to self. Are you willing to die to self?

If you have children or grandchildren, are you teaching them what a Christian life looks like?

Are you teaching your family "how to handle life skillfully?"

JOY IN THE TRUTH

"These things I have spoken to you so that My joy may be in you, and *that* your joy may be made full" (John 15:11).

T he most noticeable attribute missing in the Christian community is joy. In many churches, there are sad faces strained from worry and regret. One theologian stated, "… most Christians hang on a cross of discouragement because one hand is nailed to the worries of tomorrow and the other is nailed to the regrets of yesterday."[26] Anxiousness and remorse unhinge Christians from trusting in the sovereignty of God, and so joy, escapes them. Joy can be defined as having the deep, settled confidence that God has everything under control. Not having this confidence in God makes one unthankful for the situation. A Christian is to be thankful in all circumstances (1 Thess. 5:18) as a thankful attitude fuels joy. This anchors the fact that God has the future in His hands, and He has forgiven past, present, and future sins.

---

[26] https://www.goodreads.com: Warren Wiersbe

Joe Holland's article in *Table Talk*, February, 2017, describes four types of joy. I elaborate on each type and rename two in italics:

1) Fake joy or *Fool's gold joy* is finding joy in sin by satisfying the fleshly desires. J.R.R. Tolkien, author of <u>The Lord of the Rings,</u> wrote a letter to his twenty-one-year-old son. He wrote: "The devil is endlessly ingenious, and sex is his favorite subject. He is as good every bit at catching you through generous romantic or tender motives, as through baser or more animal ones." This is the devil's fool's gold as many have discovered in our culture's sexual revolution.

2) Fickle joy or *Fair-weather joy* is finding joy in good circumstances. For example, fair-weather fans have joy when their favorite team is always winning, but when losing, they switch to a winning team. Joy is lost once the situation is no longer pleasant. As long as life is going in a positive direction, joy abounds. When the winds shift, depression, dissatisfaction, and discouragement blow into the person's heart.

3) Fading joy – Joy fades when rooted in the materialistic. It is like the Word sown in the Parable of the Sower (Mark 4:1f). Great joy is given, but the weeds (things of the world) entangle the person to choke off joy. It is only a momentary feeling of happiness

or contentment. Examine someone's attic, garage, or storage areas, where a host of fading joy fills each.

4) Forever joy – Forever joy flows from a relationship with Jesus (John 15:11). Jesus joy creates...
   A. Joy from salvation. (Ps. 51:8-12)
   B. Joy in knowing that God sovereignly has everything under control. (Ps. 115:3)
   C. Joy in being a citizen of His kingdom. (Rom. 13:17)
   D. Joy in the strength received. (Neh. 8:10)
   E. Joy in song. (Neh. 12:43)
      1. Sing with confidence in God. (Phil. 4:13, 19)
      2. Sing of contentment in God. (Phil. 4:11-12)
      3. Sing of complete peace "of" God and "with" God. (Phil. 4:7; Rom. 5:1)
      4. Sing to celebrate Jesus. (Phil. 4:4)

Jesus taught that if one is grafted into Him and the person abides in His Word, then the individual will have the fullness of His joy (John 15:11) and the Holy Spirit's fruit of joy (Gal. 5:22). This is why the apostle John wrote, "I have no greater joy than this, to hear of my children walking in the truth" (3 John 1:4).

Questions to Consider

Are you living a "fool's gold" life of joy?

Are you living a "fair-weather" life of joy?

Is your attic or garage filled with "fading joy" items?

KNOWLEDGE OF THE TRUTH

"Reason is the devil's whore."[27] Martin Luther

"...who desires all men to be saved and to come
to the knowledge of the truth" (1 Tim. 2:4).

Every day, people are reading *The Washington Post, The New York Times, The Wall Street Journal,* or watching CNN, MSNBC, or Fox News to discover the facts of our world. For example, the stock market is influenced by what one reads or hears, and either the bull or bear market's stock reading is like an EKG analysis most days. Man is trying to reason how to keep personal finances healthy as well as the nation's economy, but reasoning without God in the equation of one's thinking makes "reason the devil's whore."

Knowledge is the key to unlocking numerous discoveries. However, mankind was created to gain knowledge through his relationship with God and viewing life through the lens of Scripture. Evolutionary theory seems to have won the day in

---

[27] https://www.goodreads.com: Luther on Reason

America's culture by eliminating God from the equation. When God is removed from the reasoning process, then creation, sin, and redemption are washed away from one's thoughts.

The origin of humanity's fall came when Adam and Eve ate from the tree of the knowledge of good and evil after being commanded by God not to do so (Gen. 2:16-17, 3:6). Once that disobedient act took place, mankind's nature was corrupted by and shackled to sin. The choice of eating from the tree was mankind's declaration of independence from God and his wanting to be like God. Mankind's choice of right from wrong must be based solely on what God has decided is right and wrong as written in His Word. When God's authority is diminished, men/women become "god." Man was created with an umbilical cord tied to God. This is why Jesus taught, "You can do nothing apart from Me" (John 15:5). When the cord was severed in the garden, humanity staked its claim in its independence.

Humanity's self-absorbed knowledge based on truthiness has tried to stabilize differences and correct wrongs by saying that humans are basically good. Improve the environment and give everyone jobs, a house, transportation, health care, and education, etc., and all will be well in the land. It is a lie! Why? The sin (selfish independent nature) of humanity is not recognized or acknowledged.

The Scripture text from the book of 1 Timothy 2:4 states that God desires for all to be saved so that they can come to the knowledge of the truth. Salvation from what? The penalty of sin! Jesus's death, burial, and resurrection are the pathway for the forgiveness of sin. The knowledge of an empty cross and tomb are the highwater marks of Christianity.

Having the knowledge of the truth opens the eyes and hearts to the sin nature of humanity and how mankind naturally responds:

+ dead spiritually – Col. 2:13
+ enslaved by sin – John 8:34
+ governed by sinful nature, controlled by the world's system, captive to the devil – Eph. 2:2-3
+ blind – Eph. 4:18
+ defiled in conscience – Titus 1:15-16
+ trapped in darkness – Col. 1:13
+ without understanding – 1 Cor. 2:14
+ hostile towards God – Rom. 5:7
+ a hater of light – John 3:19-20
+ without desire for God – Rom. 3:11
+ without fear of God – Rom. 3:18

Having the knowledge of the truth also opens the eyes and hearts to the works of the triune God: the Father, the Son (Jesus), and the Holy Spirit. God the Father chooses His kingdom residents, God the Son redeems the kingdom citizenry through His blood, and God the Holy Spirit secures the kingdom populace (Eph. 1:1-13).

God's kingdom consists of those who have come under His authority and rule. Only by having the knowledge of the truth that Jesus saves from the penalty of sin will one be put in His proper place in the kingdom—being a child, a sheep, and a slave of God (Luke 12:32).

I once read that the cross removes the *penalty* of sin, the Holy Spirit eliminates the *power* of sin, and glorification destroys the *presence* of sin. The insurrection of the original family, the first Adam, was only resolved by the resurrection of the second Adam—Jesus. Jesus will lead all of His followers to the knowledge of the truth.

Questions to Consider

Are you reasoning issues of life without God in the equation of life?

From the list of sin's natures, which ones do you struggle with the most?

What are two highwater marks of Christian knowledge?

LACK OF THE TRUTH

"Yes, truth is lacking; And he who turns aside from evil makes himself a prey" (Isaiah 59:15a).

"They bend their tongue *like* their bow; Lies and not truth prevail in the land; For they proceed from evil to evil, and they do not know Me," declares the Lord" (Jeremiah 9:3).

"For the wrath of God is revealed from heaven against all ungodliness and unrighteousness of men who suppress the truth in unrighteousness...For they exchanged the truth of God for a lie, and worshiped and served the creature rather than the Creator, who is blessed forever. Amen" (Romans 1:18, 25).

If one listens to TV talk shows like *The View* or *The Talk*, late night hosts (Fallon, Kimmel, Colbert), Oprah Winfrey, and others, they all claim their view is truth. Any other opinion is considered heresy. In fact, if a Christian voice's a different thought, he is considered narrow-minded, fundamental, or simply crazy. If you disagree with the television celebrities, the liberal news commentators, or the far-left, you become their prey. "While Paul was saying this in his defense, Festus said in a loud voice, 'Paul, you are out of your mind! Your great learning is driving you mad'" (Acts 26:24). As Paul had become the prey in his day, Christians in America today are the targeted, proving the truth of Isaiah 59:15a.

In America, we have observed the hunted: a baker, a florist, conservative political figures, and others are being dragged into the truth maligner's dungeon. Jeremiah stated that lies prevail in the land (Jer. 9:3). As in the prophet's day, lies have swept across the landscape of America, and evil is rampant in our society. The apostle Paul was clear that truth has been exchanged for a lie, and in our culture, the creature is worshipped, not the Creator.

The dam of lies has burst, and the waters of those lies are flooding our country. Who is responsible for creating this bursting dam that has caused the barrier to crumble?

First and foremost is the church. Liberal theology—not believing that the Bible is authoritative and inerrant—has caused this flood of lies to overflow our society. The church has morphed into the culture instead of the church transforming the culture.

Second, the family. Families have been more concerned about the material world than the spiritual. Comfort has led to conformity, which leads to complacency. The lack of biblical principles being lived through the family has filled our country with acceptable immorality.

Third, the educational system. Education from grade school to the university level indoctrinates students with politically correct thinking and immorality more than the basic facts in a subject area. Lies prevail through the halls of education because they lack the truth, and students come away with skewed views of history, science, biology, creation, and government, to name a few. The truth of God and the Bible are not found in the secular educational arena.

Fourth, the judicial system. From local courts to the Supreme Court, justice and righteous laws are hard to find. Legal tactics evade biblical truth. The Supreme Court weighs in cultural opinion more than righteous thinking. About sixty years ago, the Supreme Court began to reveal its hand of unrighteousness. Two prime examples are the Engel v. Vitale decision in 1962 and the District v. Schempp in 1963 decisions on banning prayer and Bible reading in school. Along with liberal churches and seminaries, these rulings were the beginning of the current erosion of righteousness in America. These are but two pseudo-truth court decisions drowning America in unrighteousness.

What can be done to reverse this flood of lies? The Christian must find the courage to bring truth back to the family, the church, and the educational and judicial systems. Through the power of the Holy Spirit, we must convey the light of God's truth to our drowning culture. THINK! While many are tubing down the river of lies, some are holding on to the life raft of the truth—they are the hunted.

Questions to Consider

If you stand for truth, it makes you prey. Does this scare you, or are you willing to stand for right?

Are you part of transforming the culture, or are you conforming to the culture?

What are the four cultural systems that are contributing to the lack of truth in America?

Morality in the Truth

"Many will follow their sensuality, and because
of them the way of the truth will be maligned;..."
(2 Peter 2:2).

"Were they ashamed because of the abomina-
tion they had done? They certainly were not
ashamed, and they did not know how to blush"
(Jeremiah 6:15, 8:12).

The 1960s saw the first wide-spread sexual revolution in
modern America. Now almost sixty years later, compar-
atively, the sixties were the kindergarten era of sexual expression. Today, people "hook-up," not even knowing the person's
name, for a sexual encounter. While cohabitation, prostitution,
and adultery became commonplace in past decades, today we
have seen the explosion of sex with children, animals, same
gender relationships, and sex trafficking.

In other words, at all cost, the sexual cravings must be
satisfied.

Many of these practices seem to thrive even in the church, with the acceptance now of same gender relationships, cohabitation, and adultery. What these actions do is malign or blaspheme the truth. One author references 2 Peter 2:2 from the website, "Precept Austin:"

> Peter says that because of the lascivious lifestyles of "so called saints" and "church goers", the watching world will judge the whole church based on their evil behavior with the result that the reputation of Christianity and God Himself are slandered and denigrated. Not only that, but the lost world smugly justifies (at least in their warped way of thinking) their own licentious behavior. They mock and scoff at the gospel of Jesus Christ because of nominal "Christians" who do not follow the Lord Whom they claim as Savior.[28]

The truth is being maligned through the character and practices of the many who call themselves Christians and churches. Sadly, though, neither blushes. People's shame is missing when they do an immoral act. No one is sorrowful when he is caught in the act or discovered. For example, celebrities and political figures whose sexual behaviors have been brought into the light publicly show no remorse. Shame is

---

[28] https.//www.preceptaustin.org: II Peter

gone when a church places a "rainbow" banner across the front of the church. Embarrassment has disappeared when couples living together are welcomed into the church. Blushing is gone when there is no repentance from unwed mothers in a church.

What has allowed the sexual revolution to accelerate in America at a warp speed? When there is no standard, when sin becomes the norm, people live only to satisfy their fleshly appetites. They are unconcerned with the things of God. The apostle John declared, "No one born of God makes a practice of sinning, for God's seed abides in him; and he cannot keep on sinning, because he has been born of God. By this it is evident who are the children of God, and who are the children of the devil: whoever does not practice righteousness is not of God, nor is the one who does not love his brother" (1 John 3:9-10). John was clear—if one practices sin, he is not born of God. The operative word is "practice." All Christians sin, many even falling into sexual sins. A Christian, however, does not "practice" or habitually sin. But if he finds himself caught in the snare of immorality, he confesses he has sinned; then he repents and ceases from the evil act. The work of the Holy Spirit brings conviction of the sin to the sinner. "If we confess our sins, He is faithful and righteous to forgive us our sins and to cleanse us from all unrighteousness" (1 John 1:9).

If the church and America continue on this path of accepting and practicing free sexual expression, then the judgement of God will come upon the nation. "As it is written in the law of Moses, all this calamity has come on us; yet we have not sought the favor of the Lord our God by turning from our iniquity and giving attention to Your truth" (Dan. 9:13). Not only will calamity fall upon our nation, but our allegiance to satanic forces will be revealed as well.

QUESTIONS TO CONSIDER

Do you blush at sin, or do you brush it off?

Is there a standard of morality? If so, where is this standard derived from?

Does the practicing of sin without feeling remorse fit the character of a Christian?

Nation of the Truth

"You shall say to them, 'This is the nation that did not obey the voice of the Lord their God or accept correction; truth has perished and has been cut off from their mouth" (Jeremiah 7:28).

"These are the things which you should do: speak the truth to one another; judge with truth and judgment for peace in your gates" (Zechariah 8:16).

"The Christian faith is not true because it works; it works because it is true. It is not true because we experience it; we experience it - deeply and gloriously - because it is true."[29] Oz Guinness

From where does a nation glean its truth? Jeremiah's prophecy, written about 2,600 years ago, is still applicable

---

[29] Os Guinness, *Time for Truth: Living free in a world of Lies, Hype, and Spin*, (Grand Rapids, Michigan, Baker Books, 2,000), p. 79.

today. Truth has perished, and it has been cut off from our country because we have not obeyed the voice of the Lord. Guinness was spot on in his assessments of truth in his book *Time for Truth,* "All truth is God's truth and is true everywhere, for everyone, under all conditions." He went on to say, "Truth does not yield to opinion, fashion, numbers, office, or sincerity – it is simply true..." [30]Our culture has replaced true-truth with opinion, feelings, experience, and/or whoever yells the loudest. This is why the Supreme Court listens to the loud static of a few people instead of the clarity of God's truth. Decision makers have allowed philosophy and opinion and not theology to oversee our nation.

In America, one might say the Declaration of Independence is the source of truth; however, the Supreme Court can interpret an issue based on popular opinion rather than from the original intent of the Founding Fathers. The glaring example is the Supreme Court's decision in the Obergefell v. Hodges case (5-4, June 2015), approving gay marriage based on the Constitution's statement of "Life, Liberty, and the pursuit of Happiness." What is missing from the Court's decision? The issue of morality. Where does one find the moral truth about marriage? Where was the institution of marriage formulated? Historically, the tradition in the United States has been that marriage is between a man and a woman. The arrangement for traditional marriage flows from the Bible (Gen. 2:24). While throughout America's history, there have been homosexuals

---

[30] Ibid., p. 79.

who are, according to the Constitution, entitled to life, liberty, and the pursuit of happiness from our government, it should not be at the expense of biblical truth.

Today, there is an under-current of Marxist ideology in our nation. These followers believe that capitalism is an evil, making this ideology unfair for the masses in America. However, capitalism has been the vehicle God has used for mankind to work and prosper and to use his God-given gift-edness for God's glory. We are to work hard to embrace a life-style that will allow for helping others through our prosperity to the glory of God. But it is not the government's role to dictate through higher taxation how much a person is to give to help others. Higher personal taxes will only stymie creativity and the enthusiasm to work. Granted, even among Christians, there is greed and a higher than necessary lifestyle, but the government is not to be the police force to correct unfairness.

The Declaration of Independence states that we are "endowed by their Creator…" The signers of the document held to a belief in God and/or biblical principles. Zechariah was right that a nation needs to speak truth to each other and judge with truth for peace to be in the land. If prosperity, security, and freedom are to be maintained in America, the nation must be a nation of the truth, not truthiness.

QUESTIONS TO CONSIDER

Has truth escaped America? If yes, how so?

Are we a nation that makes decisions from feelings or truths?

Will the work ethic of the masses reach one's potential best through capitalism or Marxism?

Overcomers for the Truth

"These things I have spoken to you, that in Me
you may have peace. In the world you will have
tribulation; but take courage, I have overcome
the world" (John 16:33).

Knowing the condition of the world, and especially the
United States, some might throw up their hands and
say, "What is the use—it is hopeless!" Watching the erosion
of America makes one's heart break. People have abandoned
the truth for a lie. The apostle John's text could be a news
headline, "Tribulation in the World!" Without a doubt, there
is tribulation in our world. Many are attempting to escape
the tribulation by searching for peace through pills, drugs, sex,
work, material possessions, social causes, etc. However, the
Christian is called to be an overcomer. Putting on the scriptural armor (Eph. 6:10f) will allow one to overcome the lie
with the truth.

First and foremost, one must put on Jesus Christ (Rom.
13:14). John was clear when he wrote, "For everyone who has

been born of God overcomes the world. And this is the victory that has overcome the world—our faith" (1 John 5:4-5). It is the faith that believes that Jesus is the way, the truth, and the life, and except through Him, no one comes to the Father (John 14:6). The apostle Paul exhorted the faithful to put on the helmet of salvation (Eph. 6:17). In addition, the faithful follower of Jesus believes that Jesus is God (1 John 5:20).

Second, salvation in Jesus promises that the third Person of the Trinity will live within the believer. "Little children, you are from God and have overcome them, for He who is in you is greater than he who is in the world" (1 John 4:4). That is to say that the Holy Spirit is more powerful and wiser than Satan. The Holy Spirit, not Satan, teaches truth. "When the Spirit of truth comes, He will guide you into all the truth" (John 16:13). Jesus's earthly life was to be lived in the shadow of the cross to obediently carry out His Father's will so the Spirit would come.

Third, the believer puts on the belt of truth (Eph. 6:14). Tethered to the belt of truth is the sword (Eph. 6:17b), which is the Word of God (Heb. 4:12), where truth is located for the believer. Again, John wrote, "...I write to you, young men, because you are strong, and the word of God abides in you, and you have overcome the evil one" (1 John 2:14). Another piece of armor, as cited in Ephesians 6, is the breastplate of righteousness (v 14b), which protects the heart. Additional armor used to fight for truth is the gospel of peace to cover the feet for firm footing (v 15) and the shield of faith to quench the fiery darts of lies (v 16).

On the battlefield of lies, the soldier of faith is exhorted not to fight underhandly while fighting for truth. In other words, "Do not be overcome by evil, but overcome evil with good" (Rom. 12:21). The "armor of light" (Rom. 13:12) has been put on, and now the warrior of the truth will walk in holiness as he is protected from the devil's temptations of fleshly desires and lies (Rom. 13:13-14). Dressed in armor for battle, the truth warrior now can be salt and light in the world (Matt. 5:13-16).

Even if heartache, pain, and maybe even death come on the battlefield, the Christian can be faithful. Throughout church history, the church flourishes when the blood of her warriors becomes the seeds to grow the truth. The faithful overcomers will be courageous people giving hope to America. For even though there is great tribulation, the warrior has great courage because he knows the Lord has overcome the world.

Questions to Consider

What tribulations do you see in the world?

With all the tribulation in world, are you living in faith or fear?

Do you dress in the armor of God daily?

Practice of the Truth

"If we say that we have fellowship with Him and *yet* walk in the darkness, we lie and do not practice the truth;" (1 John 1:8).

"But he who practices the truth comes to the Light, so that his deeds may be manifested as having been wrought in God" (John 3:21).

"The one who says, "I have come to know Him," and does not keep His commandments, is a liar, and the truth is not in him;" (1 John 2:4).

When one hears the word practice, one usually associates the word with sports. To practice is to do something repeatedly until that thing comes second nature to the person. My favorite play in all of sports is the double play in baseball. It is an athletic maneuver that requires the accuracy of a throw to second base for the first out, then an acrobatic type move around the second base bag to make a throw to first, where the first baseman usually stretches out to catch the ball for the second out. To perform this play at the professional level, many hours of practice are required to make the double play look effortless.

In the theological arena, to practice truth is similar to the meaning in sports. One has to continually repeat a truth so that it will become second nature to him. When a person is born again and regenerated, godly-life practices must be developed to replace the old habits of life. For example, instead of watching sports on a Sunday morning, the convert is in church. Athletes have an inner desire to please their coach and fans. Likewise, the new Christian's desire is to glorify the Lord. As the new lifestyle develops over time, churchgoing eventually becomes a willingly and easily undertaken action.

To react automatically to a play, a baseball player is taught to think through the game situation prior to balls being hit to him. John, in his gospel, stated that if one practices the truth, he spontaneously desires to glorify Jesus, the Light (John 3:21). The aim is to show others the new life deeds that come from God. Polar opposite is John's statement in his first letter. One cannot say he has fellowship with God and live in lies. That person is not practicing truth. Secondly, one who says, "I know Him," but fails to keep God's commandments is a liar; one who has never desired to come to the light.

Practicing truth allows one to keep God's commandments. This occurs through the sanctification process of a believer through the Holy Spirit's working in the believer's life in concert with the Word of God. Then the believer will come to love others and keep God's law instinctively.

Practicing truth gives the believer an advantage of knowing how to confront pseudo-truths. A barrage of lies is released daily through the news media. For example, according to the January 27 – February 2, 2021 *Epoch Times* (a conservative newspaper), "Ninety percent of news outlets in the United States are controlled by just six corporations. They aren't out to tell you the truth about what's happening. They paint a picture of the world that they want you to see." We are also fed lies from political arenas, Hollywood, and, sadly, even the church. The Bible is clear that numerous false teachers will be in the world. In order to distinguish between what is true and what is false, the Christian must be discerning, wise, and knowledgeable of Scripture by staying in the Word.

Most play the mind game of the "what if's" in life, which can throw people a curve ball: what if I lose my job, or what if my spouse leaves me? Consequently, they remain in constant turmoil, which can lead to depression, discouragement, and dissatisfaction. Truth turns the negative thinking into a positive outlook because one places the problem under the microscope of Scripture—truth. This is practiced by turning the "what ifs" into the "even ifs." In Daniel 3, Shadrach, Meshach, and Abednego were told they were to fall down and worship the golden image of Nebuchadnezzar or be thrown into the fiery furnace. Their response in 3:17-18, "If it be so, our God whom we serve is able to deliver us from the furnace of blazing fire; and He will deliver us out of your hand, O king. But **even if** He does not, let it be known to you, O king, that we are not going to serve your gods or worship the golden image that you have set up."

The lesson for us to learn is that we need to place our heads each night on the "sovereign pillow" of God. By practicing truth before others, they will see how effortlessly we are handling our life circumstances. This life-play of trusting God and practicing truth far exceeds the beauty of baseball's double play.

Questions to Consider

If you are "practicing" sin, are you really saved?

What are your "what ifs," and how can you turn them into "even ifs"?

Is practicing truth "effortless" for you? If not, what are your struggles? How can you overcome those struggles?

QUANDARY AROUND THE TRUTH

"Jesus Christ: a liar, a lunatic, or Lord?" C.S.
Lewis, *Mere Christianity*

"Now, therefore, fear the Lord and serve Him
in sincerity and truth; and put away the gods
which your fathers served beyond the River and
in Egypt, and serve the Lord" (Joshua 24:14).

C.S. Lewis's book *The Silver Chair* is about Jill, who is
lost and thirsty in a strange land. She finds a brook, but
she sees Aslan, the Lion (a symbol of Christ), lying beside
the brook.

Aslan growls and tells her she may come
and drink.

"May I...could I...would you mind going away
while I drink?" said Jill.

The Lion answered with a look and very low growl and as Jill gazed at its motionless bulk, she realized that she might as well have asked the whole mountain to move aside for her convenience. The delicious rippling noise of the stream was driving her nearly frantic.

"Do you promise not to do anything to me if I do come?"

"I promise," said the Lion.

Jill was thirsty now that, without noticing it, she had come a step closer.

"Do you eat girls?" she said.

"I have swallowed up girls and boys, women and men, kings and emperors, cities and towns," said the Lion.

"I dare not come and drink," said Jill

"Then you will die of thirst," said the Lion.

"Oh, dear," said Jill coming a step closer. "I suppose I must go and look for another stream then."

"There is no other stream," said the Lion.[31]

People are looking for a stream to satisfy their worldly thirst. They drink from the wells in the world and leave with their thirst unquenched, like the woman at the well (John 4). Jesus said, if you drink from Jacob's well you will always be thirsty. But if you drink from Me, you will never thirst again (John 4:13-14).

The dilemma of truth is that most do not see Jesus as Lord but as a liar—teaching lies to manipulate or maneuver people into His web of thinking and living. They see Him as a lunatic with crazy, wild, and unreasonable teachings like the cult leader Jim Jones, who had his followers "drink the Kool-Aid," killing 918 followers in 1978. The quandary, or dilemma, can be resolved by following the Joshua text 24:14, "… fear the Lord, serve Him in sincerity and truth…" But the challenge comes in putting away the gods one follows. Only then will the first part of the text come to fruition. As Lewis wrote, "There is no other stream." Until one realizes that there is nothing in the world that will douse a thirsty soul except Jesus, people will run to the streams of their god—work, recreation, sports, sex, drugs, food, etc.—to quench the inner desire for peace of the soul and life. All other gods one serves are liars. The real lunatics of life are the people who chase after these gods. Observe the number incarcerated, the many

---

[31] C.S. Lewis, *The Chronicles of Narnia, Book 6, The Silver Chair*, (New York, New York, Harper Collins, 1953

in rehab or recovery facilities, the statistics for divorces, and the high rate of suicides. One has to ask, who is really the liar and lunatic?

Jesus gave the promise, "If anyone is thirsty, let him come to Me and drink, He who believes in Me, as the Scripture said, 'From his innermost being will flow rivers of living water'" (John 7:37-38). The living water is Jesus flowing through you. These waters contain love, joy, peace, patience, kindness, goodness, faithfulness, gentleness, and self-control (Gal. 5:22). The quandary, or dilemma, of truth is resolved in Jesus. Only by kneeling beside and drinking from the stream of life, Jesus, can one experience true soul satisfaction.

QUESTIONS TO CONSIDER

How do you see Jesus—as a liar, lunatic, or as Lord? Why?

Are you drinking from the world's wells to quench your thirst, or have you learned to drink from Jesus, the living water?

Do you see living waters flowing through you as described in Galatians 5:22?

RECONSTRUCTION OF THE TRUTH

"If everything is endlessly open to question and
change, then everything is permitted, nothing
is forbidden, and literally nothing is unthinkable." [32]Os Guinness

"For they exchanged the truth of God for a lie
and worshiped and served the creature rather
than the Creator, who is blessed forever. Amen"
(Romans 1:25).

A revolution of change is in the air for America through
the reconstruction of her philosophical, theological,
and political ideologies. A reconstructionist in the culture is
one on the far-left in the three areas stated. This new era of
thought is not for the betterment of America. Philosophically,
mankind is the center of thought. Theologically, the Bible is
outdated, and God is basically dead. Politically, capitalism is

---

[32] Os Guinness, *Time for Truth: Living free in a world of Lies, Hype, and Spin,*
(Grand Rapids, Michigan, Baker Books, 2,000), p. 56.

evil, and the government is the god of the land. Guinness was spot-on when he said the flood gates have been thrust open to a plethora of "whatever's:" whatever the human, sinful mind can imagine can become a reality.

Reconstruction didn't occur overnight. Its proponents worked "below the waterline" to create a revolution in America. Their strategy reminds me of the construction of the Brooklyn Bridge. In the late 1800s, the Brooklyn Bridge in New York City was under construction. This miracle bridge took seventeen years to build. For four years, the community could not see construction above the water. Roebling, the overseeing engineer of the bridge, was criticized for not building the bridge faster. Roebling's response was epic: "Men have risked their lives building a strong foundation below the waterline. If this important work was not done below the waterline what was built above the waterline would not stand the test of time." [33] The work of these reconstructionist has been going on below the waterline for decades. However, unlike the Brooklyn Bridge's foundation, is their foundation below the waterline so secure that their ideologies will stand the test of time, and is their foundation as secure as they think?

So-called modernization, for now, is flourishing because God is no longer in the equation of a reconstructionist. These ideology advocates attempt to achieve something originating from their flesh, not from God. As the apostle Paul wrote,

---

[33] https://www.throughtout history.com: story of the Brooklyn Bridge.

"For they exchanged the truth of God for a lie..." and anything originating from the flesh is not built on a sure foundation.

Francis Frangipane, in his book *Holiness of Truth and the Presence of God*, wrote, "Sin wears a cloak of deception..."[34] and because it does, Guinness was totally correct in saying, "literally nothing is unthinkable." For example, we have seen the "unthinkable" at our southern border with people entering illegally and receiving government support and the right to vote; doctors allowing a baby to die in a steel basin after a botched abortion; some parents calling their children "theybies" during the children's first four years of life, letting the children decide what gender they will be – UNTHINKABLE!

The designers of the unthinkable, of pseudo-truth, who have operated under the waterline are found in all areas of our culture—churches, universities, Hollywood, and liberal politicians. What these institutions and individuals have done is to rework truth to exclude God—the true-truth. Without the triune God, the flesh becomes god, and it will construct the unthinkable, where everything is not only permitted but is celebrated.

Jesus stated that there are two foundations—one is made of rock, and the other sand (Matt. 7:24-27). The wise build on the rock of truth by obeying the words of Jesus, and the wise will flourish. The foolish, the reconstructionist, build on sand,

---

[34] Francis Frangipane, *Holiness, Truth and the Presence of God*, (Lake Mary, Florida, Charisma House, 2011), p. 2.

and no matter how long they work below the waterline, their foundation will not last, and it will be destroyed.

Questions to Consider

What do you see as the most "unthinkable" thing happening in America today? Without truth, how have things changed philosophically, theologically, and politically?

Will these new ideas and thought processes stand in time? Why or why not?

Suffering for the Truth

"Blessed are those who have been persecuted for the sake of righteousness, for theirs is the kingdom of heaven. ¹¹ "Blessed are you when *people* insult you and persecute you, and falsely say all kinds of evil against you because of Me. ¹² Rejoice and be glad, for your reward in heaven is great; for in the same way they persecuted the prophets who were before you" (Matthew 5:10-11).

"For we can do nothing against the truth, but *only* for the truth" (2 Corinthians 13:8).

"The blood of the martyrs is the seed of the church." [35] Tertullian

In the Scriptures, suffering is multidimensional. The apostle Paul wrote, "We are afflicted in every way, but not

---

[35] https://www.christianitytoday.com: December 4, 2014, "Sorry, Tetullian

crushed; perplexed, but not driven to despair; persecuted, but not forsaken; struck down, but not destroyed" (2 Cor. 4:8-9). Probably, each reader, whether Christian or not, can describe a season of suffering. People's suffering can have many faces; some suffer from illnesses or financial difficulties; some experience the death of loved ones; some, broken marriages or families. Any of these, or more, has probably touched your life. But what about suffering for the truth?

Throughout church history, martyrs have given their lives for the truth of the only true Triune God and the Holy Scriptures. Tertullian, (AD 160-220), the church father who lived in the midst of persecution, said, "The blood of the martyrs is the seed of the church."[36] Polycarp (AD 155), a disciple of the apostle John, said to a hushed mob before he was burned at the stake, "Eighty and six years have I served Christ, and He has never done me wrong. How can I blaspheme my King and Savior? I fear not the fire which burns for an hour, and after a little while is extinguished ...why do you delay? Come, do your will."[37] Prior to these martyred saints, the apostle Paul stated, "For I consider that the sufferings of this present time are not worth comparing with the glory that is to be revealed to us" (Rom. 8:18).

Currently, according to some experts, a pattern is emerging reminiscent of Jewish persecution in post-war Germany. "Isolation of, and discrimination against Christians is growing

---

[36] Ibid.

[37] https://www.christianhistoryinstitute.org: Polycarp testimony

almost geometrically" said Don McAlvany in "The Midnight Herald." "This is the way it started in Germany against the Jews. As they became more isolated and marginalized by the Nazi propaganda machine, as popular hatred and prejudice against the Jews increased among the German people, wholesale persecution followed. Could this be where the growing anti-Christian consensus in America is taking us?"[38]

As stated previously, America is in a truth war. Anytime there is a war, there are causalities. Why are the sufferers of the gospel willing to die? They believe, as Paul wrote, that what is beyond this world is far greater, and they desire to see all come to a saving knowledge of Jesus. Thus, believers stand tall in proclaiming and protecting the truth about God and the Bible to those who do not like to hear that they are sinners and that if they don't repent, they will be sentenced to hell. People don't want to hear that it is only through Jesus that a person can have eternal life (John 14:6). Consequently, those proclaiming truth are persecuted as unbelievers fight for their perceived knowledge of life and their goodness to others and hold fast to the idea that God is only a God of love, expecting these things to take them to heaven.

The truth is that God **is** a God of love but also a God of wrath, judgement, and punishment. The Holy Triune God cannot and will not allow sin to enter into heaven. This truth war really is around a person, Jesus Christ, His substitutionary atonement for our sin, and His resurrection. Believers

---

[38] https://www.flame.org. Christian Persecution

will continue to suffer through persecution and possibly die, holding to this truth because of their love for Jesus and others. But the paradox is that the church will flourish, as always, through the seeds of a martyr's blood.

QUESTIONS TO CONSIDER

Has the church been too complacent in our culture?

How will you stand for Christ in the midst of persecution?

Why does the church grow when Christians suffer?

TOLERANCE OF THE TRUTH

"Our lives are shaped by the 'god' we worship – whether the God of the Bible or some substitute deity." (Nancy Pearcey – *Total Truth*)

"Truth is that which is consistent with the mind, will, character, glory, and being of God. Even more to the point: Truth is the self-expression of God." (John MacArthur, "The Truth War")

"For the time is coming when people will not endure sound teaching, but having itching ears they will accumulate for themselves teacher to suit their own passions, and will turn away from listening to the truth and wandering off into myths" (2 Timothy 4:3-4).

Years ago, people could debate ideas yet part on good terms. In other words, they could tolerate a different opinion. Today, if one does not agree with a person's opinion, then he is classified as a hate monger or worse. Relativism has become a person's god. "It is my thought, so it must be true. And who are you to disagree with me?" is the thinking of the relativist. Nancy Pearcy was correct in writing that one is shaped by the "god" one worships. Although not admitting it, most worship the god of self. Even though an opinion is a lie, they believe it as truth because it fits their philosophy of life. This is where many Americans are today: intolerance must be digested by the tolerant, but tolerance is indigestible to the intolerant.

Guinness pointed out in *A Time for Truth* the relativist banner, "Truth is dead; knowledge is power."[39] He highlighted Fredrick Nietzsche's influence on the life of Picasso. Picasso's mantra was, "Truth cannot exist ...truth does not exist. I am God, I am God."[40] Nietzsche is famous for his question, "Is God dead?" which was the *Time* magazine cover headline on April 8, 1966. The erosion of the existence of God in America began in the sixties, and almost sixty years later, some believe God is dead, and many live as if He doesn't exist. The rapid increase in the "nones," those who have no religion and self-identify as atheists or agnostics, reveals the outcome of the erosion of the existence of God in America.

The book of 2 Timothy 4:4 says those who have itching ears have turned away from listening to the truth. This has happened in churches across America, and the pseudo-truth

---

[39] Os Guinness, *Time for Truth: Living free in a world of Lies, Hype, and Spin,* (Grand Rapids, Michigan, Baker Books, 2,000), p. 84.

[40] Ibid., p. 84

teachers and leaders have made their way into the universities and into the political arena. Their politically correct agenda will not tolerate the truth as defined by MacArthur.

When Jesus taught that He was God (at least thirty-eight references in the Bible to that fact), the Pharisees could not stomach such a heretical statement. Jesus stated, "Most assuredly, I say to you, before Abraham was, I AM" (John 8:58). The Old Testament scholars, Pharisees, and scribes knew that "I AM" was God because when Moses, in Exodus 3 1-17, met God at the burning bush, He told Moses to tell Pharaoh that the "I AM has sent me to free the Israelites." Jesus's truth statement, I AM, could not be tolerated, so the religious leaders had Him executed on a cross.

Colson described the worldview of our culture in his book *The Good Life*, "No such thing as truth! Tolerance is god! Diversity rules at all cost."[41] Worldview thinkers are intolerant of what they describe as the narrow-mindedness of biblical teaching. Thus, they can reprimand an employee for having a Bible on a workplace desk. The Quran, far Eastern religious literature, and other faiths are recognized in public, but not Christianity's Bible. The tolerance of truth has vanished. If politically correct language is not expressed, if agreement with abortion is contradicted, if the gay lifestyle and marriage are opposed, and any if religion allowing anyone entrance into heaven is not accepted, a Christian today will

---

[41] Charles Colson, *The Good Life*, (Wheaton, Illinois, Tyndale House Publishers, Inc., 2005), p. 225.

be called intolerant, fundamentalist, ignorant, and not relevant in today's culture. Intolerance by the worldview thinkers rules the landscape—agree or be bullied or worse.

QUESTIONS TO CONSIDER

How can you freely express your political or theological views publicly?

How is America heading toward the era of Nazi Germany?

Is your opinion always truth? If yes, why; if no, why?

UNIVERSALITY OF THE TRUTH

"Let the lie come into the world, even dominate the world, but not through me."[42] (Alexander Solzhenitsyn)

"...And everyone who hears these words of mine and does not do them will be like a foolish man who built his house on the sand.[27] And the rain fell, and the floods came, and the winds blew and beat against that house, and it fell, and great was the fall of it" (Matthew 7:26-27).

One of the great movie dialogues is from *A Few Good Men*[43] between naval lawyer Kaffee and Marine Colonel Jessup during a trial to prove that a "Code Red," (a hazing technique to motivate slack soldiers) was authorized

---

[42] Os Guinness, *Time for Truth: Living free in a world of Lies, Hype, and Spin,* (Grand Rapids, Michigan, Baker Books, 2,000), p. 19.

[43] https://www.reddit.com: movies

by Colonel Jessup. Hear the heated courtroom dialogue with
Colonel Jessup on the witness stand:

Kaffee: Colonel Jessup, did you order
the Code Red?

Judge Randolph: You don't have to answer
that question!

Colonel Jessup: [*to Kaffee*] I'll answer the question! You want answers?

Kaffee: I think I'm entitled to answers.

Colonel Jessup: You want answers?

Kaffee: I want the truth!

Colonel Jessup: You can't handle the truth!

"Truth, Veritas," the motto for Harvard University has
become a cliché or worn-out slogan. This grand university
once touted, "The end of education is to know the Lord Jesus
Christ who is eternal life."[44] Truth is no longer a highwater
mark of these higher learning institutions and so-called places
of worship. Consequently, cultures cannot handle the truth,

---

[44] https://www.webpages.uidaho.edu. Harvard

which is that the Triune God is the only Truth. All that He has said through His Word, the Bible, and all that He has created is truth. God's truth is universal in nature. God is the Truth in the Western hemisphere as He is in the Eastern hemisphere. What has happened to truth? In the East, it was trampled upon by socialism, and in the West, by materialism. People have permitted the government and materialism to be their god. In addition, in religious circles like Mormonism, Jehovah's Witnesses, and far Eastern religions, a false view of God is taught.

Is it not strange in America that there are advocates clamoring for socialism? Have they not seen the spiritual wasteland that socialism creates in other countries? Here in America, the country is becoming like a desert; we are trying to build a country on an ideology of sand. The prophetic voice of Jesus in Matthew's gospel, as stated above, could become a reality in America. In his 1978 commencement address at Harvard, Solzhenitsyn stated, "We have placed too much hope in politics and social reforms, only to find out that we were being deprived of our most precious possession: our spiritual life."[45]

All socialist nations (and all other philosophies throughout the world) are blinded to God, and America has developed cataracts which have blurred her vision of God. The universal truth is that God will rule His creation. Creation must come under submission to the Creator. In Psalm 117, the psalmist declared, "Praise the LORD, all you nations! Praise Him all

---

[45] https://www.solzhenityncenter.org: speeches

you peoples! For His merciful kindness is great toward us, And the truth of the LORD endures forever." Will our nation hold to lies or turn toward the truth? Are you living the lie or the universal truth—Jesus is God, the God of total truth? Around the world, 1+1=2. Similarly, around the world, Jesus is the universal Truth, regardless of what philosophy any nation is embracing. As Solzhenitsyn said, "Let the lie come into the world, even dominate the world, but not through me."[46]

QUESTIONS TO CONSIDER

Jesus said, "I am the way, the truth, and the life. No one comes to the Father except through Me." Is this statement true around the world, or just in America?

What has happened to truth in America and in Eastern nations?

Why is socialism replacing truth in America?

---

[46] Os Guinness, *Time for Truth: Living free in a world of Lies, Hype, and Spin,* (*Grand Rapids, Michigan, Baker Books, 2,000*), p. 19.

VOICE OF THE TRUTH

" ...and for this I have come into the world, to testify to the truth. Everyone who is of the truth hears My voice" (John 18:37).

"See to it that no one takes you captive (carries you off) through hallow and deceptive philosophy; which depends on human tradition and the basic principles of this world rather than on Christ" (Colossians 2:8).

A re the voices of this world carrying you off into darkness without your realizing it. Chuck Colson stated, "America has grown accustomed to the dark, they don't even know the lights are out."[47] Which voice are you hearing—your voice or the voice of God; the voice of relativism or the voice of truth; the voice of socialism or the voice of capitalism? Through all the murmuring noises, who are you going to trust?

---

[47] Charles Colson, *The Good Life*, (Wheaton, Illinois, Tyndale House Publishers, Inc., 2005), p. 197

Who has remained consistently trustworthy and faithful? Has socialism? Examine the economic failure, the imprisonment of those who didn't follow the government's agenda (e.g. Solzhenitsyn), and the squelching of religion.

Has relativism, whose cousins are humanism and secularism, been faithful and trustworthy? Only the loudest opinions will surface to be heard and followed. These three "isms" fail to capture the state of the human nature. Everyone is a sinner. Sinners lie to achieve their desired goals, and many times, they don't know they are lying because it is part of their unregenerate nature. Those listening believe the lie is truth. The liar is part of the devil's kingdom because he is the father of lies. What follows lies is deception. Liars are deceivers, making others think they are doing the right thing. Deception finally gets one entangled in the liar's web of ideology, philosophy, and theology. Basically, the voice of God is silenced, and humans see themselves as gods. You have been held captive through deception; you have become the spoil.

Jesus was crystal clear in His statement, "Everyone who is **of the truth** hears my voice" (John 18:37). In other words, if you have a relationship with Jesus, you will hear His voice of truth. Can the voice of God be trusted? Guinness made God's trustworthiness markedly obvious, "God may be trusted because He is the True One. He is true, He acts truly, and He speaks truly - for Christians, most clearly and fully in Jesus,

His effective, spoken Word. God's truthfulness is therefore foundational for His trustworthiness."[48]

How can one have ears to clearly hear the teachings of Jesus amidst the clamoring of the world's voices? As Jesus shared with the Pharisee Nicodemus, one must be born again (John 3). A regenerated heart removes the cataracts from one's eyes and the hearing impairments from one's ears, which frees the heart so that the voice of truth can resonate within the person. Once hearing the truth, the new believer abides in truth, and the truth sets the person free (John 8:31-32).

Now one can discern what is truth and what is a lie and which voice to trust—the One who is the Truth, Jesus.

QUESTIONS TO CONSIDER

Whose voice are you listening to for truth?

With all the static in the world, where can you hear clarity?

What are the "ism's" that are the loudest in America?

---

[48] Os Guinness, *Time for Truth: Living free in a world of Lies, Hype, and Spin,* (Grand Rapids, Michigan, Baker Books, 2,000), p. 81.

Weight of the Truth

"When Christ calls a man, He bids him come and die."[49] Dietrich Bonhoeffer

"[41] And he withdrew from them about a stone's throw, and knelt down and prayed, [42] saying, 'Father, if you are willing, remove this cup from me. Nevertheless, not my will, but yours, be done.' [43] And there appeared to him an angel from heaven, strengthening him. [44] And being in agony he prayed more earnestly; and his sweat became like great drops of blood falling down to the ground" (Luke 22:41-44).

With the words of Jesus in John 19:30, "It is finished", we saw the truth change an entire world. Because of Jesus's great love for the Father and for us, He willingly took on the weight of the cross. Jesus experienced that weight of His impending death in the garden when He prayed three

---

[49] https://www.goodreads.com: Bonhoeffer

89

times, "Father, if you are willing, remove this cup from me, yet not my will but yours be done" (Luke 22:42). That cup carried not only the wrath of God to be poured out in judgement of sin but also the excruciating soul pain Jesus would experience from being separated from His Father. In fact, the weight of what He was to endure was so intense that droplets of blood fell from His forehead as He prayed. Due to His desire to obey His Father and His love for all who would come to Him by faith through grace, He was willing to be obedient to His Father's will by taking on the weight of the cross.

From the sin Adam and Eve committed of eating the fruit from the tree of the knowledge of good and evil, a sin nature entered the life of every person born from that time on, and a blood sacrifice would be required to cover the sins of people. Yearly, in the Old Testament, the temple priests would go into the Holy of Holies to sacrifice a lamb for the people of Israel. This yearly sacrifice was ended for all time by Jesus's substitutionary atonement and sacrificial death on the cross. His blood alone satisfies the payment for all the sins of those who call on His name for salvation. The cross is the weight He endured for all who are called to believe in Him.

Three years earlier, Satan had tried to derail Jesus from going to the cross by tempting Him with lies of power, popularity, and prosperity (Matt. 4:1-11), trying to convince Jesus that a less costly way should be considered. But Jesus would not give in to Satan's temptations, refusing the easy road offered by showing through Scripture how deadly these snares would be. Jesus chose the road of obedience—the Via Dolorosa.

As Dietrich Bonhoeffer said, "When Christ calls a man He bids him come and die."[50] We will face the same lures that Jesus did from Satan; nevertheless, because of our Lord's obedience, we have been shown the way to bring truth into our world. It will cost us, as it did Him. We will need to take up our cross and follow Him; we will need to love Him more than family; we will need to be willing to die to self. We could find ourselves stereotyped, marginalized, and maybe even criminalized and persecuted, but consider Paul's words to the Romans, "For I consider that the sufferings of this present time are not worthy to be compared with the glory that is to be revealed to us" (Rom. 8:18). The weight of the cross, and all that it brought, was not enough to keep Jesus from looking to the results of His sacrifice, our salvation. Let us be about bringing the truth to a dying world as He did, regardless of the cost.

Questions to Consider

Why is the blood of Jesus the only thing that will cover your sin?

What temptations does Satan use to tempt you?

---

[50] Ibid.

Guinness said, "Living in truth is the secret of living free."[51] Do you see why this is true?

---

[51] Os Guinness, *Time for Truth: Living free in a world of Lies, Hype, and Spin,* (Grand Rapids, Michigan, Baker Books, 2,000), p. 87.

X-Factor of the Truth

Jesus is the difference Maker

In my pre-teen and teen years, I collected Major League Baseball cards. One could buy a box of a hundred cards for a dollar in the late fifties and early sixties. My collection today, if I still had the cards, would be valued at approximately $40,000. I remember buying a Willie Mays card from a friend for seventy-five cents, a large sum of money then. What made my collection so valuable were the "difference makers" in the collection. Players like Mantle, Maris, Robinson, Kaline, Clemente, Aaron, Ford, Koufax, and Drysdale are just a few examples of the difference makers in the collection. These difference makers had an X factor that made them vital to the success of their teams. But who is the all-time great difference maker in life with the X factor that changes lives? It is not a sports figure, philosopher, theologian, entrepreneur, writer, speaker, or politician. None of these! The greatest difference maker was and always will be Jesus Christ. Jesus is the

X factor in life. Jesus has the most significant impact on the outcome of true-truth because He is the Truth.

Educators have tried to eliminate Christ from the public classroom from kindergarten age to the university student. But thankfully, there are Christian teachers and campus and sport chaplains who make Jesus visible. At the campus in my hometown, a number of athletes have had a salvation experience and acknowledged Christ as their Lord because of the godly men and women devoted to telling the student athletes about Jesus.

Although numerous liberal so-called churches dot the landscape of our nation, there is a significant number of X factor churches who proclaim that "man is a great sinner in need of a great Savior."[52] These churches are making a difference in their congregations and communities for God's glory, as a multitude of people have come to Christ and are now serving Jesus locally, nationally, and globally. These have the X factor because they have a relationship with the X factor—Jesus. I baptized two Muslim medical students, and before entering the baptismal water, they wanted me to change their names to John and Mary. They are X factors as they serve the Lord through medicine today in New York City.

In story after story in the gospels, one finds Jesus affecting people like the Samaritan woman at the well, who was an adulterer or prostitute. Jesus impacted her life by telling her how to quench her thirst (John 4). Jesus came to Zacchaeus, the chief

---

[52] http://www.goodreadscom: Newton

tax-collector in Jericho, to impact his life. The tax-collector responded to Jesus's call and repaid all whom he had cheated by four-fold (Luke 19). The woman caught in adultery was about to be stoned. Jesus asked the Pharisees whichever of them was without sin to throw the first stone. Since they knew none of them was without sin, they departed, and Jesus told the lady that He did not condemn her and to go and sin no more (John 8).

How about you? Has Jesus been the X factor for you? It doesn't matter if you claim to be humanistic, secularist, atheist, or whatever you want to tag yourself as Jesus can impact your life to reveal to you real truth and real life. All you need to do is to confess your selfish independent nature and ask Jesus's forgiveness. Then trust in Jesus's love-work on your behalf through the cross at Calvary. There on that hill of suffering, Jesus exchanged His righteousness for your sin. In other words, He took upon His body all your sins and credited to your life's account righteousness. Through His blood, you are justified by His grace and through your faith. You believe Jesus was buried and that on the third day, the Father raised Him from the dead. You believe in a bodily resurrection which allows you to have eternal life in heaven and not have to face the anguish of hell. Jesus's desire is to be your X factor! Come!

QUESTIONS TO CONSIDER

Do you see how Jesus is the X factor in life?

How can you and I be X factors in the world?

Who has been the most influential person in your life? Why?

Yearning for the Truth

"But it seems that something has happened that has never happened before; though we know not just when, or why, or how, or where. Men have left God not for other gods, they say, but for no gods; and this has never happened before, that men both deny gods and worship gods, professing first Reason, and then money, and power, and what they call life, or race, or dialectic. The church disowned, the tower overthrown, the bells upturned, what have we to do; but stand with empty hands and palms upturned in an age which advances progressively backwards."[53] T.S. Elliot

"As a deer pants for flowing streams, so pants my soul for you, O God. ² My soul thirsts for God, for the living God..." (Psalm 42:1-2a).

---

[53] https://quotefancy.com: T.S. Elliot

The above statements contrast where many Americans are spiritually—some seeking the selfish, independent life, while others are yearning for God. As a nation, we live in a dangerous time of America moving "progressively backwards" toward a state of bondage. Alexander Fraser Tytler (1748-1813) wrote about a nation's life-cycle. "From bondage to spiritual faith, from spiritual faith to great courage, from great courage to liberty, from liberty to abundance, from abundance to selfishness, from selfishness to complacency, from complacency to dependency, from dependency back to bondage."[54] America has reached the complacency stage, which will lead to dependency on the government, which will lead America back to bondage.

What has catapulted us into this position? It is we, as a people, who no longer yearn for true-truth. The church is to be the pillar of truth (1 Tim. 3:15), yet the condition of our nation is muted from many pulpits.

Jesus taught the priority of life, "But seek first the kingdom of God and his righteousness, and all these things will be added to you" (Matt. 6:33). Proverbs 14:34f reads, "Righteousness exalts a nation, but sin is a disgrace to any people." Jesus was saying for us to thirst for, yearn for His righteousness and to be in a right relationship with Him. The yearning is toward the Person who can teach the truth, not a truth. Unless we reprioritize our lives, we will be a people wandering in the wilderness, thinking, "How did we get to this place?"

---

[54] https://commonsensegovernment.com: Tytler

Listen carefully! Jesus's teachings will set you free and satisfy your soul. As He stated, if we seek Him first, He will provide for, care for, and protect us. On the other end of the spectrum, people are clamoring for the government to be the provider, caretaker, and protector. That comes with a price. The price tag is higher taxes, politically correct mandatory speech, and allegiance to the government, not God. In Nazi Germany in 1935, prayers ceased in schools; only state-approved teachers taught religion; doctrines of the Bible were replaced for the dogmas of Nazism; Christmas and Easter were changed to "Yuletide" and "arrival of spring;" the swastikas replaced the cross and other symbols of the Christian church. Listen to Hitler, "Do you really believe the masses will be Christian again? Nonsense! Never again. That tale is finished. No one will listen to it again. Even the pastors will support us."[55]

Unless our nation, especially the church, yearns for Jesus—the Truth—we will find ourselves in a 1935 era of bondage. We must first seek God's authority in our lives and a right relationship with the Lord; then He will bring peace. But if we continue toward universal income, health care, and education, the socialist voices will have successfully removed God from America. Are you yearning for God, thirsting for the living God, no matter the cost? "Blessed are those who hunger and thirst after righteousness, for they shall be satisfied" (Matt. 5:6).

---

[55] https://books.google.com: Hitler

QUESTIONS TO CONSIDER

On a scale 1 (lowest) to 10 (highest), what is your yearning to know Jesus?

The promise is by seeking Jesus first, He will take care of your needs. Do you believe He really will provide for you what you need?

How satisfied are you in life? How can you be totally satisfied?

Zenith of the Truth

"Now if Christ is proclaimed as raised from the dead, how can some of you say that there is no resurrection of the dead? [13] But if there is no resurrection of the dead, then not even Christ has been raised. [14] And if Christ has not been raised, then our preaching is in vain and your faith is in vain. [15] We are even found to be misrepresenting God, because we testified about God that he raised Christ, whom he did not raise if it is true that the dead are not raised. [16] For if the dead are not raised, not even Christ has been raised. [17] And if Christ has not been raised, your faith is futile and you are still in your sins. [18] Then those also who have fallen asleep in Christ have perished. [19] If in Christ we have hope in this life only, we are of all people most to be pitied" (1 Corinthians 15:12-19).

Z enith, defined by the Oxford dictionary, is "the time at which something is most powerful or successful."[56] The most fruitful moment or powerful time in Jesus's ministry was when the tomb was empty. Yes, the cross is highly significant in the Christian faith. However, without the resurrection of Jesus, the cross would be insignificant. This is why the resurrection is the zenith of truth. The resurrection of Jesus fulfills all the promises of Scripture and the teachings of Jesus and ensures the future of the church. The apostle Paul stated that without the resurrection, our faith is meaningless and preaching is pointless (I Corinthians 15:14). Still more important, everyone would still live in his sinful nature.

The resurrection is the heart of Christianity. It is the most powerful moment in history. Of all the faiths in the world, Jesus is the only God who is living. All human gods are lifeless and cannot receive worship or offer anything. The Christian worships a living God, Yahweh, Who has given us His living Word, the Bible, and Who has granted a living hope for all who believe in His death, burial, and resurrection according to the Scriptures.

Jesus's resurrection solidifies the truth. This historical event is the glue that holds truth together. John wrote in his second letter, "For the sake of the truth which abides in us and will be with us forever." (2 John 2). He wrote the epistle for "truth" that the reader would not compromise the truth. The reason the "truth abides in us" is because a believer has the

---

[56] https:/www.oed.com

Spirit of truth, the Holy Spirit, living in him. The reason the Holy Spirit can live in a Christian is because of the resurrection of Jesus (John 16:7). The Spirit of truth will always be with the believer.

There are basically three choices about life after death. One, there is no life after death. The life one now lives is all there is. Second, reincarnation is a popular belief, where one's soul returns to the earth in a new body. Third, is the resurrection. Like Jesus, a believer will have a bodily resurrection. The resurrected body will be recognizable, incorruptible, and glorified. Which of the three after-death experiences is true?

The resurrection is the only one that can be validated because history agrees that Jesus's tomb was vacant after He was buried, and He was seen by many witnesses. The swoon theory (Jesus was drugged), the twin theory (Jesus's twin was killed), and other weightless suppositions try to disprove Jesus's resurrection, but all fail wretchedly.

The resurrection is indeed the highwater mark and the most powerful moment in history. It is the zenith of truth surrounding Jesus Christ. All true-truth hinges on this one historical event. I ask you, where are you finding truth? From politicians, liberal clergy who only believe the Bible contains truth, the media, your opinion or experience, or from a non-Christian faith? None of these offers what only the resurrected, living Lord can. Come to Jesus, the risen Lord, and He will teach you the truth that will set you free.

Questions to Consider

What is the core belief in Christianity?

What solidifies truth?

If Christ has not been raised from the dead, then we have no faith, and our preaching is in vain. True or False?

Book Resources

1) Charles Colson and Nancy Pearcey, *How Now Shall We Live?* (Tyndale Publishing, 1999)

2) Os Guinness, *Time for Truth: Living Free in a World of Lies, Hype, and Spin* (Baker Books, 2000)

3) John MacArthur, *The Truth War: Fighting for Christianity in an Age of Deception* (Nelson Books, 2007)

4) R. Albert Mohler, Jr., *Feed My Sheep: A Passionate Plea for Preaching: The Primacy of Preaching,* (Orlando, Florida, Reformation Trust Publishing, 2008)

5) Nancy Pearcey, *Total Truth: Liberating Christianity from Its Cultural Captivity* (Crossway Books, 2004)

6) Francis Schaeffer, *The God Who Is There* (Downers Grove, Ill.: InterVarsity Press, 1998)

CPSIA information can be obtained
at www.ICGtesting.com
Printed in the USA
BVHW071233290621
610722BV00003B/285